Rule of the Jesus Prayer as taught to St.

Pachomius the Great by an angel.

"An Angel of God taught St. Pachomius the Great a rule of prayer for the vast community of monks dependent on him. The monks under the spiritual direction of St. Pachomius had to perform the rule every day. Only those who had attained perfection and the unceasing prayer connected with it were freed from the obligation to perform the rule. The rule taught by the Angel consisted of the Trisagion, the Lord's Prayer, Psalm 50, the Symbol of Faith (Creed) and 100 Jesus Prayers. In the rule the prayer of Jesus is spoken of like the Lord's prayer, that is, as prayers generally known and in general use."

—St. Ignatius Brianchaninov, *On the Prayer of Jesus*

RULE FOR SAYING THE JESUS PRAYER

(this can be used as a personal rule of prayer, in addition to morning and evening prayers, and/or when one desires to increase his/her prayer – of course, the Jesus Prayer can be said at any time throughout one's life, in fulfillment of St. Paul's injunction to 'pray without ceasing')

The Trisagion Prayers

In the Name of the Father, and of the Son,
and of the Holy Spirit.

Amen.

Glory to thee, our God, glory to thee.

O heavenly King, O Comforter, the Spirit
of truth, who art everywhere present
and fillest all things;

Treasury of good things and Giver of life:

Come and abide in us and cleanse us from

every impurity, and save our souls, O good

One.

Holy God, Holy Mighty, Holy Immortal:

have mercy on us. (Thrice)

Glory to the Father, and to the Son, and to

the Holy Spirit: now and ever and unto

ages of ages.

Amen.

All-holy Trinity, have mercy on us. Lord, cleanse us from our sins. Master, pardon iniquities. Holy God, visit and heal our infirmities for thy Name's sake.

Lord, have mercy. (Thrice)

Glory to the Father, and to the Son, and to the Holy Spirit: now and ever, and unto ages of ages.

Amen.

Our Father, who art in heaven, hallowed be thy Name; thy kingdom come; thy will be done on earth, as it is in heaven. Give us this day our daily bread; and forgive us our trespasses, as we forgive those who trespass against us; and lead us not into temptation, but deliver us from evil.

Through the prayers of our holy Fathers, Lord Jesus Christ our God, have mercy on us and save us.

Amen.

Lord, have mercy. (12 times)

Glory to the Father and to the Son and to the Holy Spirit, both now and ever, and unto ages of ages.

Amen.

O, come, let us worship and fall down before God our King. (metania)

O, come, let us worship and fall down before Christ our King and our God. (metania)

O, come, let us worship and fall down before the Very Christ, our King and our God. (metania)

Psalm 50

Have mercy on me, O God, according to
Thy Great Mercy; and according to the
multitude of Thy compassions blot out my
transgression. Wash me thoroughly
from mine iniquity, and cleanse me from
my sin. For I know mine iniquity, and
my sin is ever before me. Against Thee
only have I sinned and done this evil
before Thee, that Thou mightest be
justified in Thy words, and prevail when
Thou art judged. For behold, I was
conceived in iniquities, and in sins did my
mother bear me. For behold, Thou hast
loved truth; the hidden and secret things
of Thy wisdom hast Thou made manifest

unto me. Thou shalt sprinkle me with hyssop, and I shall be made clean; Thou shalt wash me, and I shall be made whiter than snow. Thou shalt make me to hear joy and gladness; the bones that be humbled, they shall rejoice. Turn Thy face away from my sins, and blot out all mine iniquities. Create in me a clean heart, O God, and renew a right spirit within me. Cast me not away from Thy presence, and take not Thy Holy Spirit from me. Restore unto me the joy of Thy salvation, and with Thy governing Spirit establish me. I shall teach transgressors Thy ways, and the ungodly shall turn back unto

Thee. Deliver me from blood-guiltiness, O God, Thou God of my salvation; my tongue shall rejoice in Thy righteousness. O Lord, Thou shalt open my lips, and my mouth shall declare Thy praise. For if Thou hadst desired sacrifice, I had given it; with whole-burnt offerings Thou shalt not be pleased. A sacrifice unto God is a broken spirit; a heart that is broken and humbled God will not despise. Do good, O Lord, in Thy good pleasure unto Zion, and let the walls of Jerusalem be built up. Then shalt Thou be pleased with a sacrifice of righteousness, with oblation and whole-burnt offerings. Then shall they offer bullocks upon Thine altar.

The Creed (The Symbol of the Faith)

I believe in one God, the Father Almighty, Maker of heaven and earth, and of all things visible and invisible; And in one Lord Jesus Christ, the Son of God, the Only-begotten, Begotten of the Father before all worlds, Light of Light, Very God of Very God, Begotten, not made; of one essence with the Father, by whom all things were made: Who for us men and for our salvation came down from heaven, And was incarnate of the Holy Spirit and the Virgin Mary, and was made man; And was crucified also for us under Pontius Pilate, and suffered and was buried; And the third day He rose again, according to the Scriptures; And ascended into heaven, and sitteth at the right hand of the Father; And He shall come again with glory to judge the quick and the dead, Whose kingdom shall have no end. And I believe in the Holy Spirit, the Lord, and Giver of Life, Who proceedeth from the Father, Who with the Father and the Son together is worshipped and glorified, Who spake by the Prophets; And I believe in One Holy Catholic and Apostolic Church. I acknowledge one Baptism for the remission of sins. I look for the Resurrection of the dead. And the Life of the world to come.

Amen.

100 Jesus Prayers

LORD

JESUS

CHRIST

have mercy

on me.

LORD

JESUS

CHRIST

have mercy

on me.

LORD

JESUS

CHRIST

have mercy

on me.

LORD

JESUS

CHRIST

have mercy

on me.

LORD

JESUS

CHRIST

have mercy

on me.

LORD

JESUS

CHRIST

have mercy

on me.

LORD

JESUS

CHRIST

have mercy

on me.

LORD

JESUS

CHRIST

have mercy

on me.

LORD

JESUS

CHRIST

have mercy

on me.

LORD

JESUS

CHRIST

have mercy

on me.

LORD

JESUS

CHRIST

have mercy

on me.

LORD

JESUS

CHRIST

have mercy

on me.

LORD

JESUS

CHRIST

have mercy

on me.

LORD

JESUS

CHRIST

have mercy

on me.

LORD

JESUS

CHRIST

have mercy

on me.

LORD

JESUS

CHRIST

have mercy

on me.

LORD

JESUS

CHRIST

have mercy

on me.

LORD

JESUS

CHRIST

have mercy

on me.

LORD

JESUS

CHRIST

have mercy

on me.

LORD

JESUS

CHRIST

have mercy

on me.

LORD

JESUS

CHRIST

have mercy

on me.

LORD

JESUS

CHRIST

have mercy

on me.

LORD

JESUS

CHRIST

have mercy

on me.

LORD

JESUS

CHRIST

have mercy

on me.

LORD

JESUS

CHRIST

have mercy

on me.

LORD

JESUS

CHRIST

have mercy

on me.

LORD

JESUS

CHRIST

have mercy

on me.

LORD

JESUS

CHRIST

have mercy

on me.

LORD

JESUS

CHRIST

have mercy

on me.

LORD

JESUS

CHRIST

have mercy

on me.

LORD

JESUS

CHRIST

have mercy

on me.

LORD

JESUS

CHRIST

have mercy

on me.

LORD

JESUS

CHRIST

have mercy

on me.

LORD

JESUS

CHRIST

have mercy

on me.

LORD

JESUS

CHRIST

have mercy

on me.

LORD

JESUS

CHRIST

have mercy

on me.

LORD

JESUS

CHRIST

have mercy

on me.

LORD

JESUS

CHRIST

have mercy

on me.

LORD

JESUS

CHRIST

have mercy

on me.

.

LORD

JESUS

CHRIST

have mercy

on me.

LORD

JESUS

CHRIST

have mercy

on me.

LORD

JESUS

CHRIST

have mercy

on me.

LORD

JESUS

CHRIST

have mercy

on me.

LORD

JESUS

CHRIST

have mercy

on me.

LORD

JESUS

CHRIST

have mercy

on me.

LORD

JESUS

CHRIST

have mercy

on me.

LORD

JESUS

CHRIST

have mercy

on me.

LORD

JESUS

CHRIST

have mercy

on me.

LORD

JESUS

CHRIST

have mercy

on me.

LORD

JESUS

CHRIST

have mercy

on me.

LORD

JESUS

CHRIST

have mercy

on me.

LORD

JESUS

CHRIST

have mercy

on me.

LORD

JESUS

CHRIST

have mercy

on me.

LORD

JESUS

CHRIST

have mercy

on me.

LORD

JESUS

CHRIST

have mercy

on me.

LORD

JESUS

CHRIST

have mercy

on me.

LORD

JESUS

CHRIST

have mercy

on me.

LORD

JESUS

CHRIST

have mercy

on me.

LORD

JESUS

CHRIST

have mercy

on me.

LORD

JESUS

CHRIST

have mercy

on me.

LORD

JESUS

CHRIST

have mercy

on me.

LORD

JESUS

CHRIST

have mercy

on me.

LORD

JESUS

CHRIST

have mercy

on me.

LORD

JESUS

CHRIST

have mercy

on me.

LORD

JESUS

CHRIST

have mercy

on me.

LORD

JESUS

CHRIST

have mercy

on me.

LORD

JESUS

CHRIST

have mercy

on me.

LORD

JESUS

CHRIST

have mercy

on me.

LORD

JESUS

CHRIST

have mercy

on me.

LORD

JESUS

CHRIST

have mercy

on me.

LORD

JESUS

CHRIST

have mercy

on me.

LORD

JESUS

CHRIST

have mercy

on me.

LORD

JESUS

CHRIST

have mercy

on me.

LORD

JESUS

CHRIST

have mercy

on me.

LORD

JESUS

CHRIST

have mercy

on me.

LORD

JESUS

CHRIST

have mercy

on me.

LORD

JESUS

CHRIST

have mercy

on me.

LORD

JESUS

CHRIST

have mercy

on me.

LORD

JESUS

CHRIST

have mercy

on me.

LORD

JESUS

CHRIST

have mercy

on me.

LORD

JESUS

CHRIST

have mercy

on me.

LORD

JESUS

CHRIST

have mercy

on me.

LORD

JESUS

CHRIST

have mercy

on me.

LORD

JESUS

CHRIST

have mercy

on me.

LORD

JESUS

CHRIST

have mercy

on me.

LORD

JESUS

CHRIST

have mercy

on me.

LORD

JESUS

CHRIST

have mercy

on me.

LORD

JESUS

CHRIST

have mercy

on me.

LORD

JESUS

CHRIST

have mercy

on me.

LORD

JESUS

CHRIST

have mercy

on me.

LORD

JESUS

CHRIST

have mercy

on me.

LORD

JESUS

CHRIST

have mercy

on me.

LORD

JESUS

CHRIST

have mercy

on me.

LORD

JESUS

CHRIST

have mercy

on me.

LORD

JESUS

CHRIST

have mercy

on me.

LORD

JESUS

CHRIST

have mercy

on me.

LORD

JESUS

CHRIST

have mercy

on me.

LORD

JESUS

CHRIST

have mercy

on me.

LORD

JESUS

CHRIST

have mercy

on me.

LORD

JESUS

CHRIST

have mercy

on me.

Ending Prayers

Through the prayers of our holy
Fathers, Lord Jesus Christ our God,
have mercy upon us and save us.
Amen.

Glory to God for all things!

Made in the USA
Las Vegas, NV
01 May 2024